THE WORLD OF
Andy Capp

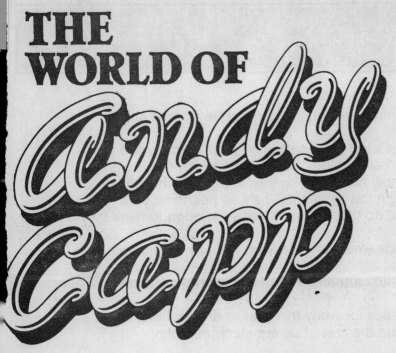

HAD A FUNNY DREAM LAS'NIGHT, PET —

CARTOONS BY
REG SMYTHE

Mirror Publications

INTRODUCTION

It isn't that Andy doesn't *want* to buy Flo a Christmas present, it's just that he doesn't know what to get her. So he says.

And Flo's put a stop to him just giving money – she's still got a couple of I.O.U.'s from years past.

Like most husbands, he finds gifts for the wife a real problem. Last year, for instance, he finally hit on a nice new scarf – only to realise he didn't know her size. The year before he thought about a washing machine but didn't want to lumber her with the payments –he's all heart really.

I don't think women appreciate gifts for the home, do they? They're selfish enough to think they should have all those things anyway.

You can't blame 'em, I suppose. After all, husbands wouldn't exactly take kindly to finding a new kettle or a tea set in *their* Christmas stockings.

Well, folks, as you'll see from this latest collection of cartoons, Flo and Andy are still battling on, as usual.

Flo has thrown no less than three going-away parties for Andy this year and each time, at the last minute, he refused to go. So it looks as if Flo and the rest of us are stuck with him.

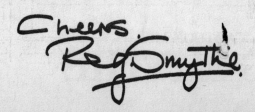

SHEESH! WHEN I LOOK AT HER NOW I'M SURE GLAD I MARRIED FLO....

I'M OFF! IF YOU HAD ANY SORT OF FEELING FOR ME AT LEAST YOU'D *TALK* TO ME!

BAR

- V196

YOU CAN'T WIN WHEN EVEN YOUR SILENCES ARE MISUNDERSTOOD

HELLO THERE, LUCY, YOU'RE LOOKING WELL

I'M ON THIS GREAT NEW DIET, FLO—

IT WAS HARD AT FIRST, MIND, BUT I'M STICKING TO IT RELIGIOUSLY AND THE POUNDS JUST ROLL OFF

V197

LOVELY. HOW LONG HAVE YOU BEEN ON IT?

SINCE YESTERDAY

THE *WILL*POWER

TRUST *YOU* TO DELAY ME WHEN I'M RUNNING LATE FOR WORK!

YOU'D BETTER GO ON WITHOUT ME, RUBE. HE'S DECIDED TO TRY SOMETHING NOVEL FOR BREAKFAST — FOOD

BORN TO BE AWKWARD

V218

HIC

V219

HI'YER, CHALKIE

ANDY! AM I GLAD TO SEE YOU — I'VE BEEN WANDERING AROUND LOST FOR AGES —!

?

WHEN THAT LAD'S ON THE MOVE, HOME IS ALWAYS IN THE OPPOSITE DIRECTION

V222

V223

V228

PREPARE YOURSELF FOR THE WORST—!

THAT COULD MEAN ANYTHING — HE COULD BE LEAVING OR HE COULD BE STAYING

Smythe

V229

PAY-DAY, PBT—!

TCH! THE STATE OF THESE NOTES

THEY'VE CERTAINLY BEEN AROUND—

THERE MUST BE A VERY INTERESTING HISTORY ATTACHED TO THEM, IF ONLY IT COULD BE TOLD

MY PART IN THEIR HISTORY WOULD BE PRETTY BRIEF — 'HERE IT IS, THERE IT GOES'

Smythe

DO YOU THINK YOU SHOULD BE WATCHING THAT SORT OF STUFF?

V244

I'M AN ADULT MARRIED WOMAN, BUT IF IT OFFENDS YOUR DELICATE SENSIBILITIES I'LL SWITCH IT OFF

HE'S GOT HANG-UPS ABOUT EVERYTHING EXCEPT HIS CLOTHES

Smythe

IF I GET MY MITTS ON YOU--!!

GRRRR

IT'S NICE TO BE NEEDED

V245

Smythe

V248

♪ DEAR OLD PALS -!!

GET Y'SELF HOME, LAD. RESPECTABLE PEOPLE ARE IN BED THIS TIME OF THE MORNING

I NOTICE YOU HAVEN'T GOT YOUR HEAD DOWN -!!

TEMPER

JACK, THE VICAR WON'T LET OUR SUPPORTERS CLUB USE THE CHURCH HALL FOR THEIR MEETINGS ANYMORE -

V249

THEY CAN BE A BIT NOISY, BUT COULD YOU POSSIBLY ACCOMMODATE 'EM?

BY ALL MEANS, ANDY -

ONLY TOO WILLING TO HELP. LET ME FILL YOUR GLASS -

SOMETHING ABOUT A CROWD LIKE THAT BRINGS A LUMP TO HIS WALLET

✡◎✪-!!

FLO, FLO, CONTROL YOURSELF. A LITTLE DECORUM, *PLEASE* —

V264

LOOK, HOW CAN I WALK OUT ON GOOD TERMS? IF I WAS ON GOOD TERMS I WOULDN'T BE WALKING OUT, WOULD I?!

SEE WHAT I MEAN?

Smythe

ARE YOU FREE FOR BINGO, FLO?

BE RIGHT WITH YOU, RUBE —

YOU HAVEN'T FINISHED THE PAINTING — THAT WOODWORK NEEDS A SECOND COAT

V265

SO DO I, BUT I HAVE TO WAIT FOR IT!

Smythe

THEY CAN TWIST ANYTHING

KEEP YOUR VOICE DOWN, MUM. HE'S GOT A BAD HEAD AFTER THE STATE HE GOT INTO LAS'NIGHT

V266

I SAW HIM, FLO. I ASKED HIM IN FOR A COFFEE AS HE STAGGERED PAST MY PLACE. HE WAS REALLY GRATEFUL AND ACTUALLY *TALKED* TO ME

YOU'LL NEVER BELIEVE WHAT HE TOLD ME, FLO—

WHAT?

WHISPER WHISPER WHISPER

YOU CAN RELY ON HER TO KEEP YOUR SECRETS—THEY'RE NOWHERE NEAR AS LURID AS HER OWN INVENTIONS

IF YOU FEEL LIKE JOINING ME FOR A NIGHT OUT, PET—

V267

HUH! AFTER ALL THE WORRY AND UPSET YOU'VE CAUSED ME THIS WEEK?!

C'MON, PUT YOUR BEST COAT ON AND DON'T FORGET YOUR HANDBAG

THAT'S *MY* LAD. IF HE'S DONE ANYTHING TO BE ASHAMED OF HE'S ALWAYS WILLING TO FORGIVE AN' FORGET

V274

V275

V282

I THINK I'M IN LOVE WITH FLO. I JUST CAN'T GET HER OUT OF MY MIND—

ANDY—!!

V283

I'M JUST POPPING OVER FOR THE RACING PAPER, FLO — HANG ON FOR TEN MINUTES

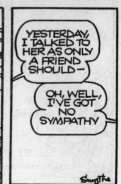

ENA'S TREATED US, PET. SHE GOT ENGAGED TO BE MARRIED LAS'NIGHT

THANKS, ENA. CONGRATULATIONS—

V302

I THOUGHT SHE HATED MEN, FLO...

SHE DOES. BUT THIS IS THE FIRST ONE THAT ASKED HER TO MARRY HIM

SOUNDS LIKE MINE

Smythe

V303

LOOK, FLO, I KNOW YOU'RE TRYING TO HELP—

Smythe

V308

IT WAS A PERFECTLY FAIR TACKLE, TWIT — YOU WERE JUST TOO FAR AWAY TO SEE!

.... I'LL CHECK WITH THE LINESMAN —

BEFORE YOU ARGUE WITH THAT LAD, BE SURE OF YOUR FACTS — THEN LET THE MATTER DROP

V309

THE THINGS YOU SAY, I HOPE YOUR WIFE ISN'T FOND OF LISTENING IN

NOT HALF AS MUCH AS SHE IS FOR SPEAKING OUT

IT'S NEVER TOO LATE TO START, MATE. GET Y'SELF DOWN TO THE JOB CENTRE—

V310

BUT HOW ABOUT FLO — SHE'S SO USED TO HAVING YOU ROUND THE HOUSE...

=SIGH=

WHAT A BLOKE COULD MAKE OF HIS LIFE IF ONLY HE WASN'T ALWAYS THINKING ABOUT OTHER PEOPLE—

Smythe

OKAY, PET?

OKAY. BUT YOU'LL HAVE TO CUT DOWN — I'M JUST NOT GETTING BY ON MY WAGES THESE DAYS

V311

WHAT'S THAT, PET?

FORGET IT

WHEN IT COMES TO PREACHING ECONOMY TO TO MY BLOKE YOU MAY AS WELL START BY SAVING YOUR BREATH

Panel 1: WHAT'S NEW, FLO? WHO'S HE CHASING AFTER AT THE MOMENT?

Panel 2: NOBODY LATELY, RUBE. THERE'S NO WAY HE COULD FIT ANY FANCY BIT INTO HIS VERY BUSY DAILY ROUTINE —

Panel 3: EVEN IF HE COULD *FIND* ONE AT HIS AGE! HEH! HEH—!

Panel 4: OH-OHH

Panel 5: ENOUGH'S ENOUGH —I'M OFF!! / BUT, PET—

Panel 6: YOU'RE WASTING YOUR BREATH —I'M GOING BACK TO MY MOTHER!

Panel 7: THAT'S BETTER THAN HER COMING HERE, EH, ANDY? HEH! HEH! HEH—!

Panel 8: SORRY, ANDY. I WAS JUST TRYING TO HELP

Smythe

HE HAS THIS RARE ABILITY TO REMAIN SILENT UNDER THE MOST VICIOUS VERBAL ATTACK—

W32

— UNTIL HE FINDS OUT FOR SURE IF THE REFEREE IS GOING TO BOOK HIM OR NOT

HERE'S THAT ARTICLE ON HOW TO CONVERT YOUR ATTIC INTO A POOL ROOM, ANDY

W33

THANKS, ED ...PHEW! TCH, TCH—

OH, NO... TCH, TCH—

POOR FLO—!

Smythe

MAY I JOIN YOU, DEAR?

SORRY, BUT I DON'T TALK TO STRANGERS

JACKIE TELLS ME YOU'RE A MARKET RESEARCH INTERVIEWER — A LASS LIKE YOU MUST TALK TO LOTS AND LOTS OF STRANGERS —

TRUE. BUT WITH A BLOKE LIKE YOU I'M NOT A LASS LIKE ME

WHAT GETS INTO 'EM, JACK?

SEARCH ME

W40 Smythe

MY DAD WAS RIGHT ABOUT YOU! IF ONLY HE WAS HERE TO SEE YOU NOW!

LET'S HEAR IT — WHAT WOULD HE HAVE TO SAY?

W41

YOU REALLY WANT TO KNOW?

CERTAINLY

THUMP

HE WAS NEVER MUCH OF A TALKER

W54

HE'S ALWAYS WILLING TO FACE FACTS — DRINKING ISN'T A SPECTATOR SPORT

W55

WHATEVER'S THE MATTER, PET?

OH, JUST ONE THING ON TOP OF ANOTHER. I HAD A REAL HORRIBLE DAY AT WORK—

NEVER MIND, PET. THERE'S ALWAYS ME TO COME HOME TO

WAAH

I'M GETTING REALLY WORRIED ABOUT CHALKIE —

THERE'S SOMETHING RADICALLY WRONG — THAT'S TWICE THIS MONTH HE'S SAID HE'D RATHER STAY IN THAN GO OUT

W58

OH, DEAR, DEAR. REALLY *IS* CRACKING UP, ISN'T HE?

HOW'S YOUR BIG ROMANCE GOING, SON?

IT'S STILL *ME* MAKING ALL THE RUNNING, MISTER CAPP

THAT'S HOW IT GOES, LAD —

W59

I WAS THE SAME. YOU WEAR Y'SELF OUT TRYING TO CATCH SOMEONE YOU COULDN'T GET AWAY FROM IF YOU TRIED!

WANNA BET?

IT'S NEVER EASY, EH, JACK?

WHAT?

DECIDING WHICH ONE TO WALK HOME ...

JUST LOOK AT 'EM —

THE POOR LAD'S ALWAYS SPOILT FOR CHOICE — THERE'S NO PLAIN WOMEN AT CLOSING TIME

W70

YOU DID RIGHT TO TELL ME, MUM. MIND YOU, I DON'T BLAME ANDY AS MUCH AS I BLAME *HER*

KEEP IT TO YOURSELF, FLO, WE'RE NOT SUPPOSED TO KNOW — DON'T GO BLABBING IT TO EVERYONE

W71

SHE ALWAYS DEMANDS SECRECY — SHE RESERVES THE PLEASURE OF TELLING EVERYBODY FOR HERSELF

GOOD GAME, PERCY?

GREAT, VICAR—

I REALLY ASSERTED MYSELF FOR ONCE. I GAVE CAPP TWO VERY STERN WARNINGS AND EVEN THREATENED TO SEND HIM OFF

W 80

Smythe

GOOD F' YOU HOW DID HE TAKE IT?

VERY NICELY, HE *FORGAVE* ME

THE NEW PEOPLE ARE JUST MOVING IN, PET—

W81

THEIR FURNITURE LOOKS DEAD CHEAP AND THEIR CLOTHES LOOK REAL SHABBY—

I'LL GO AND SAY HELLO TO HIM, PET

I THOUGHT HE MIGHT — UNDER A TATTY COAT YOU USUALLY FIND A BLOKE WHO LIKES HIS PINT

Smythe

COULD *YOU* OBLIGE ME, NIGEL?

ME? I'M STILL PAYING OFF THE WAR DEBT

W82

I'VE NO SYMPATHY FOR YOU. IF YOU'D LISTENED TO ME, YOU'D HAVE MADE PEACE AND STUCK IT OUT WITH HER AND NOT ENDED UP PAYING ALIMONY

Smythe

THEY DON'T ALL HAVE YOUR MORAL FIBRE

QUI-ET

IF RUBY CAN AFFORD A NEW COOKER I DON'T SEE WHY *WE* CAN'T

NOT YET, FLO. BEST WAIT A FEW YEARS AND THEN BUY ONE — THAT WAY WE'LL BE ONE UP ON HER

W83

BUT RUBE'S ALREADY GOT ONE—!

YES, BUT IN FIVE YEARS TIME OURS WILL BE *NEW*, EH?

Smythe

ANDY—

...FORGET IT, MATE—

W90

IF ONLY HE HAD A BETTER NATURE I COULD APPEAL TO

DO YOU THINK IT'S RIGHT TO BE OUT PLAYING GAMES WHILE FLO'S SLAVING AROUND THE HOUSE ?!

W91

I TRUST MY MISSUS — I KNOW SHE'LL WORK JUST AS HARD AS IF I WAS THERE WATCHING HER

NOSEY CAT

'BYE, FLO

LOVELY TIME, FLO

THANKS, FLO. SEE YOU

'BYE, FOLKS. MIND HOW YOU GO

GREAT PARTY YOU PUT ON, PET. I DON'T KNOW HOW YOU DO IT

THE SECRET IS JUST TO KEEP THE RELATIVES WHO DETEST HIM AWAY FROM THE RELATIVES WHO ARE A BIT UNDECIDED

W94

MUM SAW YOU TONIGHT. SHE'S BEEN ROUND AND TOLD ME EVERYTHING—

IT'S UNBELIEVABLE THE THINGS YOU GET UP TO—!

I GUESS IT IS, PET—AND AT MY AGE, TOO

W95

HIS BIG HEAD IS THE ONLY THING THAT KEEPS THIS LAD ON LIVING TERMS WITH HIMSELF

WHENEVER IT COMES TO ECONOMY IT'S ALWAYS THE BLOKE WHO HAS TO GIVE SOMETHING UP

THAT SHUT YOU UP, DIDN'T IT?

W96

WELL, THE ONLY THING I DO IS WORK — I COULD GIVE THAT UP IF YOU LIKE

HAVE YOU NOTICED? AS SOON AS THEY'RE BEAT FOR AN ANSWER THEY GET NASTY

Smythe

MY MISSUS IS ALWAYS MAD AT ME THESE DAYS, ANDY, I CAN'T OPEN MY MOUTH...

I JUST SEEM TO GET ON HER NERVES — I DON'T KNOW WHAT TO DO, I REALLY DON'T...

W97

WELL, FOR A START, I'D STOP SAYING YOU FIRST MET HER IN AN ANTIQUE SHOP —

Smythe

=SIGH=

HAPPY, DEAR?

VERY. I'M THINKING ABOUT THE WONDERFUL BLOKES IN MY LIFE

REALLY? SUCH AS?

THERE'S MY FATHER, MY BROTHER, AND POSSIBLY MY NEXT BOYFRIEND—

LOOK, I'LL PAY YOU BACK FOR THE DRINKS AS SOON AS MY MISSUS COMES IN!

W100

FANCY A CUP O' TEA, RUBE?

BE RIGHT WITH YOU, FLO

I'M GOING DING-DONG ON MY OWN—I HAVEN'T SPOKEN TO A LIVING SOUL FOR DAYS

W101

YOU'VE GOT A HUSBAND, FLO—

LIKE I SAID, I HAVEN'T SPOKEN TO A LIVING SOUL FOR DAYS

Smythe

SAME AGAIN, JACK — AND ONE FOR THE LASS AT THE END OF THE BAR

YOU BOUGHT BIG MARY A DRINK — DON'T DENY IT!

I WAS JUST TRYING TO BE FRIENDLY. ANYWAY, I DIDN'T BUY HER A DRINK — YOU DID

W130

MUST BE A BIT SAD, PARTING WITH A PIGEON

NOT AT ALL—

WHEN YOU'VE BEEN IN THE GAME AS LONG AS I HAVE, LAD, YOU GET HARDENED TO IT

WAH

W131

W134

THE SNOOKER TABLE'S FREE, ANDY —

A DROP IN THE INTEREST RATE

Smythe

W135

COULD YOU LET ME HAVE AN EXTRA FIVER POCKET MONEY, FLO? I'VE GOT A FEW EXPENSES THIS WEEK —

NO CHANCE

COME OFF IT, PET. I WOULDN'T ASK IF IT WASN'T IMPORTANT

LOOK, MATEY, I'M THE WAGE EARNER AROUND HERE AND I MAKE THE DECISIONS —

AND I'VE DECIDED TO GIVE YOU AN EXTRA FIVER

GRRR

Smythe

I'M WAITING TO LOCK UP, ANDY. GET WALKING

YOU'RE THE BOSS. LEAD THE WAY —

W136

I SHOULD'VE BEEN A BONE SPECIALIST — I'VE GOT THE HEAD FOR IT

I'M SURE I DIDN'T SPEND *THAT* MUCH. WOULD YOU CHECK THIS SHOPPING BILL FOR ME, PET?

W137

I HAVEN'T GOT A LOT OF TIME —

OH, GOOD, GOOD —

HIS BRAIN IS ALWAYS AT IT'S SHARPEST WHEN HE'S COUNTING THE MINUTES TO OPENING TIME

W144

W145

W150

W151

W166

SORRY TO HEAR ABOUT YOUR BROKEN ROMANCE, HELEN —

DON'T REMIND ME, FLO. I'M DRINKING TO FORGET EVERYTHING THAT HAPPENED

DON'T OVERDO IT, GIRL. I ONCE WENT BACK HOME TO ANDY ONLY A COUPLE OF HOURS AFTER I'D WALKED OUT ON HIM FOREVER

HEH! HEH! I'D BETTER WATCH IT, EH?

W167

YOO-HOO, FLO! CAN I COME IN?

NOT AGAIN, SURELY?

LOOK, IF MUM'S POPPING IN A BIT TOO OFTEN FOR YOUR LIKING, WHY NOT BE MAN ENOUGH TO TELL HER SO?

FORGET IT

SHE'D LIKE ME TO TAKE THE BULL BY THE HORNS AND THE BULL TO GET SLIGHTLY THE BETTER OF IT

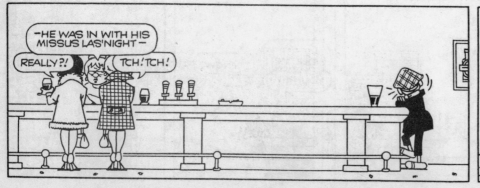

TCH! THE STUPID WAY YOU BET ON A HORSE, FLO —

YOU'RE SUPPOSED TO STUDY THE FORM, HOW MUCH IT'S CARRYING, THE GOING. YOU DON'T PICK A HORSE JUST BECAUSE IT LOOKED AT YOU —

Smythe

CORRECT ME IF I'M WRONG — IT DID WIN, DIDN'T IT?

THAT'S NOT THE POINT!

OH, HI'YER, PET. STILL UP —?

W183

Smythe

SHE DOESN'T GET AS MAD AS SHE USED TO — SHE OPENS THE DOOR BEFORE SHE THROWS ME OUT

Smythe

THUMP

WHAT'VE YOU BEEN UP TO, ANDY?

INTERRUPTING

W194

WE COULD SETTLE MOST OF OUR TROUBLES BY DISCUSSION IF ONLY I COULD GET HER TO STOP TALKING

W195

POOR LASS. I HATE TO SEE HER LIKE THIS, ALWAYS ON THE GO —

IT WASN'T ALL THAT BAD A TACKLE, WAS IT, PERCY?

NOT AT ALL

W200

WHEN YOU'VE BEEN KICKED BY HIM AS OFTEN AS I HAVE IT'S REALLY A COMFORT TO BE BRUISED IN A NEW PLACE

Smythe

COULD YOU CHANGE A TAP WASHER FOR ME, MISTER CAPP?

W201

IT'LL HAVE TO WAIT TILL I'VE CHANGED THAT FUSE FOR MISSUS POTTS—

AND CHANGED THAT POWER PLUG FOR MISSUS EVERITT—

SUITS ME

AND I'LL HAVE TO CHANGE MY IMAGE! THEY'VE CAUGHT ON TO THE FACT THAT I'M LAZY ENOUGH TO DO THINGS RIGHT THE FIRST TIME

Smythe

TCH! A MAN COMES HOME AND NO SUPPER ON THE TABLE—

W202

I'VE A GOOD MIND TO GO AND HAVE IT OUT—!

I'M WITH *YOU*, KID —CHINESE OR INDIAN?

YOU LOOK A BIT TIRED, PET

W203

I'VE BEEN DOING A LOT OF THINKING

I'VE TOLD YOU BEFORE, YOU DO FAR TOO MUCH THINKING—THERE'S NOTHING MORE WEARING. JUST YOU CUT IT OUT

MY THOUGHTS ALWAYS WORRY HIM—THEY MAY BREAK INTO WORDS AT ANY TIME

W214

I DON'T KNOW WHAT WE ARE GOING TO DO ABOUT THIS ELECTRIC BILL. IF WE DON'T PAY IT SHORTLY WE'LL BE SITTING IN THE DARK~!

I KNOW IT'S A BIT OF A WORRY, SWEET'EART —DON'T DWELL ON IT...

TELL YOU WHAT, GET YOUR COAT ON, PET, AND WE'LL POP OVER TO THE PUB FOR A QUICK ONE—

THAT'S HIS SOLUTION FOR MONEY WORRIES — GO OUT AND SPEND A BIT MORE

IF YOU'D CUT DOWN ON YOUR DRINKING WE COULD AFFORD A NEW CARPET—

AND THE STATE OF THE LINO UNDER THIS TABLE — I DON'T KNOW WHY I BOTHER CLEANING IT—

SLAM

EVERYTHING'S WEARING OUT — INCLUDING HIS NERVES

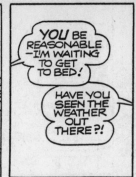

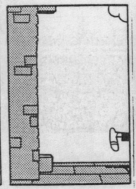

© 1988 Mirror Publications Ltd.
First published in Great Britain by Mirror Publications Ltd., Irwin House, 118 Southwark Street, London SE1 OSW.
Printed in Great Britain by Spottiswoode Ballantyne Printers Ltd., Colchester and London.
Distributed by IPC Magazines, Circulation Sales and Distribution, London.

ISBN 1 85386 138 3

the Perishers
OMNIBUS

By Maurice Dodd

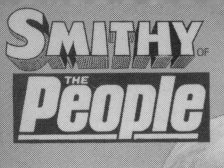

SMITHY OF THE People

My Mate CHALKIE

NEW

NICE ONE, JOHN!

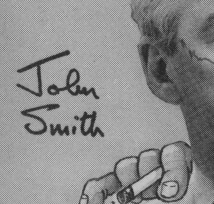

John Smith

AND FINALLY. . .